GW00870402

The FIRST *Habit*

BY LEWIS SCHIFF

BirthingOfGiants.com • 520 White Plains Road, Suite 500 • Tarrytown, NY 10591
questions@birthingofgiants.com

Cover photo: Evan Yamada

The First Habit

is dedicated to those of you

who create success on your own terms.

I've always been enthralled

by the way you live your lives.

You've given my language focus and purpose.

—Lewis Schiff

The
FIRST
Habit

Table of Contents

Discover all three habits at
BirthingOfGiants.com/3habits

What Is the First Habit?

"CREATE TWO GROUPS OF FIVE. LINE UP ALONGSIDE EACH OTHER and face the person across from you," the meeting facilitator chirped at us inside a lower-level hotel room in San Jose, California. It's a better-than-nice hotel conference room with yellowish-golden tones. Incandescent bulbs light the room, giving it a warm feeling even though there are no windows. The drapes alongside the wall where windows would be, that's the dead giveaway. Pull back that curtain and there's nothing but plaster. We've all been in this room a thousand times. And we've all had this facilitator, too. Usually he's good-looking enough, with nice teeth and an athletic build underneath his studied "business casual" attire. The kind of person who has translated his nonspecific attractiveness and cheery nature into a career where we don't mind looking at him while he helps us figure stuff out.

This meeting took place ten years ago. The other nine people in the room had already been my colleagues for a few years at this point. They weren't exactly my cup of tea back then, and even now I keep in touch with only one of them. What I didn't understand, however, is that three of these co-workers were about to change the course of my life.

"OK," said the facilitator, Bob, "here's what I want you to do. I want you to look across at the person facing you in the other line, and I want you to tell that person what you think he or she is particularly good at. Then he or she should do the same for you—tell you what you're good at. When you're done, move down to the next person and do the same thing. Do it with all five people."

So we do. The first person, Patty, says to me, "You ask good questions."

Hmm, I never thought of myself as being a particularly good listener but, OK, sure, whatever. I forget what I told her she's good at. To be honest, I forgot what I told them all.

"Switch people," Bob says.

"You're good at asking questions," Henry says to me. Again with the questions. That's weird.

"Switch."

"You're really good at technology, keeping up with the newest thing," says Frank. Now that makes sense. I'm the COO of a virtual company. I'd better be good at technology.

"Switch."

Sharla: "You always ask really good questions."

Mind blown.

Three of the first four people tell me the exact same thing. (I forgot what the fifth person said. At this point my mind is reeling.)

I had *never, ever* thought about how I ask questions. It had never occurred to me that I was a good question-asker. I'm opinionated. I like to talk. I really like it when people pay attention to me. But asking questions? If you told me to list my positive attributes at work, I doubt "asking questions" would have appeared *anywhere* on my list.

But three out of five people I'd worked with for over three years told me that I was good at this. I was speechless. For a while, anyway. Then I started asking a lot of questions.

I read once that Hemingway didn't so much write as he let "the angels move his pen." Since that exercise Bob ran us through more than ten years ago, I've come to realize the same thing is true for me. Angels drop questions into my head and then they come out of my mouth. What was once a complete mystery to me is now the way I make a living, and I'm never happier, never more engaged, than when I'm asking someone questions. That's not true. I'm never happier than when I'm asking an interesting person questions. It's not fun asking questions when the person I'm talking to is not interesting—especially if they're not interesting to themselves.

You'd think that being a questioner is a positive thing, because everyone likes to be around people who show interest in them. But being a questioner has its downsides, too. I love to ask questions so much that people tell me they feel like they're being interrogated. I've learned to compensate over time. When

I'm in a store, buying something interesting, like a new gadget, I usually start my conversation with the salesperson like this: "I'm what they call a 'fact finder.' I love to ask questions. So if you feel like I'm leaning in too close or my questions are coming at you too fast, please let me know. It just means I'm interested and excited. I don't mean to invade your space." Figuring that out took many awkward encounters.

Looking back on that day in the hotel conference room over a decade ago, I remember how amazed I was to learn that I came across as a person with a particular talent that I had no idea I possessed. But I've since come to find that this is common. When you're really good at something, you aren't aware of it, or if you are, you don't understand why it's such a big deal, why everyone can't do it. This may be the most important insight you get from this book. You probably have a talent or gift that you truly enjoy flexing, but you have no idea that it makes you different from most of the people around you. Because, to you, it feels totally unremarkable. In fact, it feels completely natural.

Since that day in San Jose, I've helped thousands of people discover their gift and hone it into a career. That's what I had to do for myself, too. After all, where in the classifieds section does it say, "Help wanted: Someone who asks lots of questions. Please provide references." If it did, I could have provided tons of references, because apparently everyone else knew this about me. Meanwhile, I was busy trying to keep up with the latest technology, learning how to manage people, becoming an expert in the minutiae of finance (or trying, at least). But since I received this thunderbolt of information in a line of five of my peers during a session facilitated by Bob, I've...

- Written several books.
- Started two education companies.
- Lectured around the world on "behavioral entrepreneurship"—this is the study of decision-making with regard to business building. It's a discipline I believe I've helped uncover and define.

Most importantly, I've come to realize that this will be my life's work: asking questions and then translating the answers for others who don't ask questions as well as I do but who, when they have those answers, can do amazing things with the information.

Today, I call this "my language." It's the way I communicate with the world. Not uniquely—after all, there are other people who ask questions well, even better than I do. But in my part of the world, entrepreneurship, I feel like I'm one of the best and, what's more, I like doing it.

What's your language? What are you really good at? Better than most people around you? And can you create a career or business around that? This is the question raised in this short book, and it's the single most important habit for you to cultivate if you want to find fulfillment and success in your work.

I've interviewed over 1,100 entrepreneurs, including some very famous ones. And they all have this one habit in common. To varying degrees, they've all built businesses around their language—every single one of them. That's why I call it "the first habit." You can't achieve your most important business goals if you don't start with this one.

But why do I call it a habit? For one, because it's something you have to keep working on to hone and develop. When I heard three of my colleagues say I was good at asking questions, I wasn't really sure what I was hearing. Was this just a comment about my personality? Or was this my language, the way I want to interact with the world? Of course, I didn't even know about the idea behind having a language, so I had to learn what *having a language* was while I figured out mine.

And second, it's an ongoing habit because I had no idea how to turn a language into a career. I'm an entrepreneur and always have been. So the question for me was, what kind of businesses am I going to build that allow me to speak my language while creating wealth and impact? As I wrote earlier, there were no job listings that were looking for questioners when I first discovered my language. Over time, I would come to understand my language like this: How do I get my head to speak regularly and truthfully with my heart while also getting my inner life to align with the outside world? And how would I do all that in the service of my life's purpose here on Earth? That probably sounds like a lot, and I have a long way to go toward achieving that, if I ever do. But that's my North Star: bringing my head and heart, my inside life and the outside world into alignment by learning and living my language. That's the purpose of my working life. And truly, I'll be OK if I never fully get there, so long as I get to keep trying for as long as I can. If I ever do arrive at that point, I want to spend as much time there as possible

So how do you get started learning your language? Well, let's keep it really simple and see if you can catch the same lightning in a bottle that I did in that hotel conference room in San Jose more than a decade ago. Send an email to ten business associates with the following message:

> *"I'm interested in your opinion about something. I want to learn more about myself and how I add value to the work that I do. You and I have worked together in the past and you've had a chance to see what I'm good at and what I like to do. Can you tell me what you think I am best*

at, given the work we've done together?"

Who knows, perhaps, like me, the answer will just appear and you can begin the heavy work of turning your language into your business. On the other hand, as I've learned through doing thousands of interviews, there are plenty of obstacles—behaviors, customs, traditions, superstitions and fears—that prevent us from learning our language or acting on it, even if we know what it is.

That's behavioral entrepreneurship. It's not just for people who want to build their own businesses; it's for people who want to bring their own language into the way they deliver value in the workplace.

Over the past few decades, the word *entrepreneur* has gone from being an insult ("He became an entrepreneur because he couldn't get a real job.") to a symbol for a desirable lifestyle. But what does it really mean to be an entrepreneur today? Let me tell you what I think it means. It means earning a living through your language; adding value to whatever enterprise you're part of—whether it's social, public sector or private—by bringing your own unique value. Perhaps you're great at developing relationships or seeing the big picture, creating high-level strategy or marshaling the efforts of technical people to get the job done. Whatever your language, there's not going to be a job listing with those words on it. No "Big Picture Expert Wanted" ad has just been posted on Craigslist. Nope, you're going to have to behave entrepreneurially if you want to bring your language to the workplace. You're going to have to define it, refine it, make sure the value it creates is evident and make sure you're being valued for that value you create. Call it intrapreneurship, disrupting, innovating or anything else. I call it entrepreneurship in the 21st century.

But first you have to learn your language. That's why I call it "the first habit," because all the challenging work ahead starts with this one question: What are you exceptional at that has to do with how you make money?

The First Habit is a practical book. It endeavors to take concepts—often ones that are expressed without much thought—and translate them into actions, which can ultimately lead to a change in your habits. Thus, the rituals of writing things down, placing them in plain sight where you will run into them every day and asking you to break big goals down into smaller, incremental steps are all designed to make you think differently and, eventually, behave differently. It's easy to find the work mundane. I've written about the perils of mundanity in the past. Mundanity is one of life's greatest enemies against progress. When things feel boring, rote, unspectacular, they can come to feel like burdens without reward, and nobody likes that. Many of the people who start this work won't finish it. They will be lulled into complacency or feel anxious because of the stirrings this work can create. Or perhaps their friends and colleagues will try to talk them out of becoming too different from the person they are today.

These are the perils faced by all who seek to improve themselves. But for those of you who push through and rewire your brain to take advantage of the truths contained inside, I believe the potential rewards include business success, which can allow you to spread your impact around the world in positive ways. If you're like me, it's not enough just to learn your language and have success; you've also got to better the quality of life here on Earth for others. Also, if you're like me, your most dynamic place to discover your language is in the world of business, a discipline that encourages creativity just as exciting as if we were painters staring at a blank canvas.

So let's create your masterpiece...

IMPORTANT NOTE ABOUT THE DATA IN THIS BOOK

This book incorporates research conducted by my friend and trusted advisor, Russ Alan Prince, from two books we worked on together: *The Middle-Class Millionaire* and *Business Brilliant*. Both of these books were built around original surveys of U.S. households designed by Prince. For the first survey, in 2006, we contacted 3,714 heads of households and asked them a series of questions about how they live their lives, access healthcare, raise their children, choose their homes and communities, and participate in philanthropy. This was the basis of *The Middle-Class Millionaire*. For our second survey, we contacted 800 households, asking them about how they made important career and wealth-building decisions. For that survey, which was explored in depth in *Business Brilliant*, the household income/net worth breakdown was as follows:

800 Households Surveyed

	Middle Class ($50k-$80k annual income)	Middle-Class Millionaire ($1mm-$10mm net worth)	High Net Worth ($10mm-$30mm net worth)	Ultra High Net Worth ($30mm+ net worth)
NUMBER	394	223	114	73
PERCENTAGE	49%	28%	14%	9%

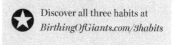
Discover all three habits at
BirthingOfGiants.com/3habits

Step One:
You Need a Plan

First and foremost, successful people are willing to learn about themselves. They learn what they want in life and they learn to set goals to attain it. They learn not to leave their future fortune and happiness to chance. They learn what they're good at and what they're not good at. They learn to use their strengths to their advantage. They learn to keep their weaknesses from getting in the way.

From Our *Business Brilliant* Survey

Agree or Disagree: "Do what you love and the money will follow."

Middle-class survey respondents who agree: 75 percent

Self-made millionaires who agree: 2 percent

Succeeding begins with one simple condition: **that you want to.**

This might not come as a surprise to you, but I've found that it's a surprise to a lot of people. As you saw above, our surveys discovered that three-quarters of middle-class Americans agree with this saying: "Do what you love and the money will follow." Many people take it on faith that loving your work naturally invites wealth and success.

It's a nice sentiment. But it's not the way self-made millionaires think. Among people who have actually achieved financial success in their lives, hardly any of them believe wealth comes as a natural reward for doing work that you love. To be exact, I found that 2 percent of self-made millionaires agreed with this idea.

This is not to say that you won't make any money if you have passion for your work. People with a sincere devotion to a calling often support themselves very comfortably. And if the main thing you want from your work is a steady paycheck large enough to provide for your retirement, it's a fine idea to do what you love and let the money follow.

From Our *Business Brilliant* Survey

"At some point in my working life, it was important for me to leave a career that was personally fulfilling in order to pursue greater financial success."

Self-made millionaires survey respondents: 65 percent agree

Middle class survey respondents: 20 percent agree

But those who have created wealth will tell you that big money doesn't just follow anything or anyone. Wealth comes only to those who pursue it.

Plenty of self-made millionaires love their work, but they don't make career decisions on the basis of lovability. They choose projects, jobs and careers that offer the strongest prospects for financial reward. Our surveys consistently show that about two out of three Self-Made Millionaires say this basic decision was important to their success.

They were determined to get rich first. Then they took the path most likely to lead them there.

So do you want to get rich? Forget for the moment how you'll get there. Just ask yourself this: Are you ready to make this important choice for yourself and your family?

What does "wealthy" look like?
The journey to riches begins by having a long-term vision of what level of wealth you want to achieve.

It can be this simple: In ten years, how rich do you want to be? What kind of life do you want?

This is no idle exercise in fantasy. People who actually create wealth tend to have a pretty good answer to this question.

That's because the pursuit of wealth requires a lot of decision-making. Choosing wealth demands that you make choices about how you spend your limited time and attention. The more successful you get, the busier you get. You have more important choices to make. Self-Made Millionaires constantly have to weigh the benefits and risks of short-term gains versus long-term investments. When is the right time to take a risk? Or to take some risk off the table?

There are no right or wrong answers. There are only decisions that are right for you at any given moment. So you need to have a long-term vision of wealth to help you decide. You need to make the choices you think are most likely to help fulfill your vision.

It's just not enough to say that you want to be a millionaire. The word "millionaire" is too vague, and there are a vast number of popular misconceptions about what a million dollars will buy. Since we were kids, we'd ask, what would you do if you had a million dollars? It's been a magic number for so long that we've stopped looking at it for what it is.

Any rich person will tell you that having a million dollars doesn't make you rich. One million dollars very safely invested will generate about $40,000 per year in interest, more or less. That's not a figure that spells financial security.

Many people think that if they had a million dollars they would no longer have financial worries. My colleague, Russ Alan Prince, has studied this. One of his surveys discovered that a lot of women were willing to marry a man they didn't love if that man had a net worth of $1.5 million. In earned interest, that amounts to just $60,000 a year. Like most people, the women in that survey never bothered to do the math.

So before you even try to picture how much money you want, take a look at this thumbnail hierarchy of wealth in contemporary America. This is a rough sketch, based on years of work with high-net-worth individuals, of how three fairly common levels of wealth are usually earned and enjoyed these days. (I'll put aside the lifestyles of multi-multimillionaires and billionaires for the moment.)

Entry-Level Millionaire ($1-3 million net worth)

With an income between $200,000 and $300,000 per year, an entry-level millionaire has a nice lifestyle that is not extravagant. About two-thirds of entry-level millionaires own their own businesses or are in professional partnerships, such as law firms and doctors' practices. If you are an entry-level millionaire, you may save and invest about $50,000 of your annual income, but that still leaves you with enough cash to enjoy first-class vacations and rejuvenation excursions, such as spa visits and adventure travel, a collection of things you care about and pricey extracurricular activities for your children. You likely have a second home in a vacation spot.

Small-Business Millionaire ($3-10 million net worth)

Owners of private companies with revenues under $50 million make up a significant share of America's millionaire population. As a proprietor of a prosperous small business, most of your net worth is tied up in the business itself. You pay yourself $700,000 a year or more, of which you save and invest about $100,000. The rest goes to first-class airfare, clothes, jewelry, watches, more extravagant collections, $500 dinners and a vacation budget that might total more than $50,000. Your social life may include philanthropy and civic leadership activities.

Multimillionaire (above $10 million net worth)

It takes at least $10 million in net worth to live what might be popularly regarded as a "millionaire lifestyle." Multimillionaires are often extremely successful corporate chieftains or business owners who have sold one privately held business for a big payout and then moved on to start another. With an annual income of about $1 million, you're likely to save and invest more than a quarter of that amount each year. Your primary home is worth at least $3 million and you might own three or four other properties for vacations and as condos for adult children or other relatives. You don't just collect art, wine or automobiles—you are a well-known "player" in whatever collecting you take up. You're a player in philanthropy as well. You donate $50,000 or more per year to your favorite causes, and sometimes you chair fundraising efforts and put on lavish fundraising events.

What's Your Vision?

Very few of the people in these three groups just stumbled into these lifestyles. Every small-business-millionaire, for instance, had to make critical decisions involving risk and reward that enabled him or her to move up from the ranks of the Entry Level Millionaire. On the other hand, many Entry Level Millionaires are currently stuck on career paths that will block them from advancing much farther unless they consciously choose to take on certain additional risks with their careers.

From Our *Business Brilliant* Survey

Survey respondents who say they have set personal financial goals:

Self-made millionaire survey respondents: 68 percent

Middle-class survey respondents: 32 percent

That is why it's absolutely essential to begin your plan to get rich by choosing a long-term vision of what you want from your lifestyle. The ten-year vision of wealth that you choose today can start giving shape and context to each and every money decision you make tomorrow.

And you must write it down. As the old saying goes, a vision that isn't written down is just an idle wish.

Think for a moment what you've already written down during the course of today. Perhaps you jotted down an important message or noted something you mustn't forget. Well, your ten-year vision for your future should be as important as remembering to pick up a quart of milk on the way home, shouldn't it?

So grab a Post-it note and write this down: *In ten years I want to have* _____.

Stick it here:

Do you realize what you've done? You've given voice to your dreams. You've just taken a tangible step that most people—maybe 95 percent of them—avoid taking for their entire lives. Everyone fantasizes about riches, but you've made a direct and firm connection between the life you have now and the life you want in ten years. You're on your way!

You might think that a Post-it® is just another scrap of paper, easily forgotten or discarded during your busy day. On the contrary, the Post-it is an essential tool for getting things done. Think about what Post-its are typically used for:

- Remembering important messages
- Capturing crucial to-do items
- Keeping a grocery list

Most of us use Post-its for those things we can't let slip through our fingers. The same is true for your ten-year vision that you just wrote down on that Post-it. You just made a promise to yourself, a "Post-it Promise." Self-made millionaires know their goals. They can recite them on demand. When you envision your important goals while reading this book, write each one down as a Post-it Promise. Make them as important as your grocery list or returning an important phone call. Treat them as something you must get done in order to be successful.

From Our *Business Brilliant* Survey

Survey respondents who say they have personal financial goals and have written them down:

Self-made millionaires survey respondents: 48 percent
Middle-class survey respondents: 17 percent

At the end of each step, you'll move all your Post-it Promises to your ***Post-it Promise Roadmap***. That's another great aspect of Post-its. As technology goes, the Post-it is a beautifully simple innovation. Putting your goals onto Post-its instead of writing them down in the pages of this book will allow you to do two crucial tasks.

First, as you reach your goals, you can remove the old Post-it Promises and replace them with new ones. Second, you can easily move all your Post-it Promises to your Roadmap, which will allow you to see how each one affects the other. With your Post-it Promises in hand, you've got the essential tool to begin rewiring your brain with new success habits.

Build Your Goals

Once you have your ten-year personal vision of wealth, you will need some shorter-term goals to help motivate you toward that vision. I suggest you look ahead five years. What do you want to accomplish in the next five years that will contribute to your ten-year vision? What set of concrete financial goals will keep you faithful to that vision?

Self-made millionaires are goal-oriented people. They crave targets to shoot for, because they use goals as tools. A goal forces you to focus. It gives you the criteria to determine what you want to work on and what it's worth to you.

One business owner I interviewed admits that he's never put together a formal business plan. He does, however, keep a close watch on his many goals. "I have a book that I look at every morning when I wake up," he says. "It has personal, long-term and short-term goals, with charts of how I plan to make those goals. I have a bar chart for sales goals. And every day, I look to see where I am and I strategize."

To get started on achieving your new vision of wealth, you will need to set a series of intermediate goals for raising your annual income. Challenging yourself to achieve an annual percentage rise in income can be a strong motivator. It's what you will need sometimes to push past the day-to-day obstacles to your vision.

Let's say you make $75,000 a year right now, and in ten years you want to be a Small Business Millionaire. You might want to start pursuing projects that will raise your income by 40 or 50 percent per year for the next five years.

That's a big step, but it's not enough. Remember that the typical Small Business Millionaire got rich by starting and growing a business that generates millions in sales each year. Given the size of your vision, merely raising your income will not get it done. You have to increase your income in ways that put you in line for owning a business that will grow and, most important, is profitable.

Right from the start, your vision and goals are helping you shape the next steps you need to take. Time for another Post-it Promise.

Write this down on a Post-it note and stick it here:

Over five years, I will
raise my income _____ percent a year,
toward my ten-year vision of achieving
(from your first Post-it Promise).

Making millions is no fantasy to a Self-Made Millionaire. Your challenge is to embrace the reality that you are on your way. Read back your Post-it Promise when you get bogged down along the way. Keep in mind that when you work your way through this new habit, you're going to be making some of the biggest leaps of your life.

What if my goals change?
Goals always change, and they tend to get bigger. Stay with this goal for a while and

you will see it happen. Once your plan starts to take root, new opportunities will pop up, ones you never would have seen until you made your first leap.

The story of Debra Lin provides a good example of how it happens. For years, Lin sold self-made jewelry in her off hours while working as a marketing manager for Mattel, the toy company, in Southern California. Back in 1985, when she earned just $8,000 from jewelry sales, her goal was a simple one. She decided that once her jewelry income equaled half her six-figure salary at Mattel, she would quit her job and run the jewelry business full time. It took her five years to reach that goal.

Once she was on her own, however, Lin realized that her income could only go so high as a do-it-yourselfer. She set new goals and started recruiting other women to sell her jewelry at parties in their homes, like Tupperware or Mary Kay cosmetics. She also rebranded the company with her childhood nickname and her maiden name—Cookie Lee. Today, 40,000 women are selling jewelry made by Cookie Lee, Inc., and the company's annual sales exceed $125 million.

Like Lin, you may find after a while that your initial income goals were too modest. Then you'll need to take some time to dream some new numbers and make a new Post-it Promise, which isn't a bad problem to have. The best way to celebrate your success is to set new goals with a renewed vision of your destination.

On the other hand, you may notice that halfway through the year, you're failing to reach your first income goal. Believe it or not, this is a good problem to have. You can use that moment to take a critical look at your skills, your field, your associates and your work habits. Setbacks are a crucial ingredient of success. I will keep repeating that throughout this book, because it can't be stated enough. Your goals often do you the most good when you are in danger of failing to meet them.

This is why you've got to start today by writing down your vision, however unprepared you might feel. Jim McCann, founder of 1-800-Flowers, said it well in his book, *Stop and Sell the Flowers:* "Don't try to know everything beforehand. If I had known everything about the flower business before I bought the first store, I never would have signed up. Sometimes you need to start down a road before you can see where it leads you."

Think of what it takes to climb a mountain. You see the peak from a distance. That is your vision, what you wrote down when you made your first Post-it Promise. But in order to make the climb, you have to get on the mountain. And on the mountain you can't see the peak. It's always obscured by one ridgeline after another. All you can do is focus on reaching that next ridge, that next goal. The peak didn't go away just because you don't see it. It's there, waiting for you.

Aren't There More Important Things In Life Than Money?

This is an inevitable question, and it leads back to why I wrote this book. Our survey research has showed us two important things about middle-class Americans and money:

1. Most of them believe they would be happier if they had a lot more money.
2. Most of them display beliefs and behaviors that will prevent them from ever making a lot more money.

I found that only 13 percent of middle-class Americans agree with the statement "Money can't buy happiness." About two-thirds of middle-class Americans believe that "without money you can't really enjoy life" and that "money is important to my personal happiness."

From Our *Business Brilliant* Survey

Top reasons for becoming wealthier, given by middle-class survey respondents:

94 percent	To achieve financial independence
93 percent	To be better able to deal with problems when they arise
87 percent	To take better care of people I care about
84 percent	To achieve greater control over my life

So you'll have to forgive me for suggesting that one way to happiness begins by setting goals for making more money. I'm only responding to what our data tells us. Most people believe it's easier to be happy with money than without it.

Are they correct? Well, in the simplest terms possible, no one can dispute that money buys you options in life that are unavailable to people without money. Having some of those options at your disposal can help make you happy. Not having options can make you very unhappy.

Don't forget, also, that if time is money, as they say, then taking control of your money goals means taking control of your time, too. Let's go back to Debra

Lin, the jewelry entrepreneur, for a moment. She was a typical high-achieving marketing executive in 1990, when she quit her job to sell her jewelry full time. Everyone around her, including her parents, thought she was crazy to forsake her years of education and corporate experience to go out on her own.

But her corporate job was extremely demanding. Her time was not her own. She often worked nights, weekends and on out-of-town trips, all at her company's bidding. Starting Cookie Lee, Inc., proved to be the path to riches for Lin, but in the short term it was also a way for her to gain more control of her daily schedule. The year Lin quit Mattel to work on her jewelry business full time was also the year she had the first of her two children. Sixteen years later, in 2007, she boasted to her local newspaper that she had never missed a school function or special event involving her children.

Some surveys suggest that women own almost half of all the small businesses in America. No doubt this desire for control of their time and their incomes, away from the corporate rat race, plays a part in the decision made by many women to strike out on their own. Not all of them are self-made millionaires, of course. Some are on their way, and some will never get there. But if making more money generally requires certain sacrifices, it doesn't mean that having more money and having a better quality of life are mutually exclusive concepts.

There's a popular saying that no one ever declared on his deathbed that he wished he'd spent more time at the office. That may be true, but it's also true that there are many retirees living hand-to-mouth today. Many had their retirement accounts devastated over the past decade and have had to consider returning to the working world. Many wish they'd made different decisions about money earlier in life. The choices they made when they were younger have deprived them of certain options that would have made them much happier now.

From Our *Business Brilliant* Survey

Today I work for myself.

Self-made millionaires: <u>83 percent</u>   Middle-class: <u>23 percent</u>

Our surveys suggest that a lot of bright, talented people will meet with similar disappointment and regret in their later years unless they change their wealth-building habits. The three that matter most are learning what you're best at, continually refining what you're best at through the practice of persistence and creating a network around you that operates on a wavelength similar to yours—goal-oriented, risk-tolerant and committed to each other's success.

Most people aren't setting goals for themselves. They're not learning how to make the most of their abilities. They're not putting themselves in situations where they stand to earn more from their efforts. They don't work on their self-development or leverage the work of others. They get discouraged far too easily, walking away from difficulties before they have a chance to learn from them. And they get pulled away from success and toward failure by the limiting beliefs of those around them.

Above all, too many of them believe that if you simply do what you love, the money will follow.

In the next chapter, I'll take that saying and stand it right on its head.

Do what you're **best** at—and then follow the money.

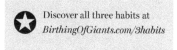
Step Two:
Zero In, Double Down

If you haven't caught on by now, I'll repeat it. The surest way to create wealth is this: First decide what you're good at. Then find the highest possible compensation for doing it.

Try reading that again. This is what you should try to do every day if you want to get rich. It should be your daily credo, your mantra.

But like any pledge or promise, it's an ideal you want to reach for. It will serve as your guiding light when you face difficult business decisions. And if you're doing it right, as we'll see, you will always be facing difficult business decisions.

Later in this book, I'll show you just how much more focus you can maintain once you keep this simple idea in the forefront of your mind: Keep dropping time-wasting tasks that are best done by others. Then use that newfound time to find better ways to make money from what you do best.

This is much easier to say than to do. It can involve a good bit of effort. As Thomas Edison used to say, "Opportunity is missed by most people because it is dressed in overalls and looks like work."

From Our *Business Brilliant* Survey

"Cutting back on expenditures helps you accumulate wealth and achieve financial success."

Self-made millionaires: 13 percent agree   Middle-class: 73 percent agree

---

Are there easier ways to get rich? Of course there are. I know a number of self-made millionaires who have gotten very rich without ever adhering to such an explicit discipline.

Or you can simply marry rich, invent a cure for the common cold, inherit millions from a long-lost uncle. Or you can win the lottery.

You can even do what so many self-help books recommend: Cut your household expenses and reinvest the savings in stocks and real estate.

From Our *Business Brilliant* Survey

Percentage of self-made millionaires who created wealth through business ownership: 94 percent

Percentage of self-made millionaires who created wealth through stock market investing: 0 percent

---

Most of the middle class seems to believe that socking away savings and investing it is an important way to get wealthy. The trouble is, while saving money can help you maintain your lifestyle in your retirement years, very few people who've attained significant wealth suggest that this is how they got there.

The reason is pretty simple. Despite all the get-rich-quick propaganda out there, the stock market and the real estate market are both very competitive games. It is obvious now, in a way that wasn't quite so obvious a few years ago, that even experts in stocks and real estate can get eaten alive when the markets turn.

If you go to a website called 2millionblog.com, you will see an excellent example of a growing genre of homespun websites that follow this creed of careful saving and self-directed investing. The blog also displays the inevitable pitfalls of such an approach to getting rich.

The 2millionblog.com site is run by an anonymous 37-year-old engineer who works for IBM in Raleigh, North Carolina. In August 2005, he claimed that he'd set a goal of $2 million in liquid assets, which represented "financial freedom" for him and his wife. He wrote: "I feel this is the perfect high-level goal that will enable me to lead an upper middle-class life without meaningful financial worries and free to pursue my life's passions and opportunities."

The blog gives every detail of the family's economic life. His wife drives a 14-year-old car. He delights in finding coupons and bargains at stores and restaurants. After reading a do-it-yourself book on trimming their pet schnauzer's coat, the couple now saves $17 per month in dog-grooming costs. They gave up cable television and their telephone landline in the same month.

All these savings and sacrifices are turned into investments toward their $2 million goal. They have maxed out all of their tax-free retirement vehicles, which is a very reasonable thing for anyone to do. Much of the rest of their savings are dedicated to playing the stock market and owning several houses that they have put up for rent.

The plan worked well for a time, and then it started unraveling. By March 2009, the plunging stock market had driven the blogger's net worth down to $400,000, all the way back to where it was in December 2007. For the all the scrimping, saving and running around looking for bargains, he made no progress at all toward his $2 million goal in more than a year.

Embracing what you do best—and finding ways of doing it that make the most money—is the *surest* path to getting rich. If they were asked for their advice, most self-made millionaires would probably tell this IBM engineer that if he wants to meet his $2 million goal, he should turn off his blog and start planning to get rich as an engineer.

That's because when you're doing the thing you do best, even when you go through rough times, you're still gaining experience and developing expertise in your most highly valued activity. I call this process "learning your language," but it goes by a lot of other terms, too. It's all about identifying your strengths, your core competencies, your special abilities. It amounts to uncovering the things you are capable of that also create value for other people.

From Our *Business Brilliant* Survey

Number of things I'm exceptionally good at that make money.

Self-made millionaires: 2.6 moneymaking skills (average)
Middle-class: 5.9 moneymaking skills (average)

This is the path taken by everyone from Bill Gates to the Beatles. It's also the path taken by some of the most successful self-made people in your own city or town. Through trial and error, they have all found the few things they are best at, cut back on distractions and diversions, and done those few things in ways that earn them the best monetary rewards.

You already have a vision of what getting rich looks like to you. You have your short-term financial goals. Now comes Learning Your Language—figuring out the way to hit those goals.

That goal of raising your income next year—by 30 percent, 40 percent or more...

Ask yourself: *How the heck am I going to do that?*

Get Yourself Centered

To learn your language, I recommend a simple three-part self-evaluation method that helps you identify your strengths, line them up with your opportunities and recognize whatever weaknesses you have that might stand in your way. (If you are already in business for yourself, you should try doing #3 first).

#1. Make a short list of your strengths. Write down several examples of things you think you do exceptionally well. This seems like a painfully simple task, but most people go their entire lives without ever doing it.

Your list may start out fairly long: "I'm good with people." "I speak well." "I've got experience in this." "I'm technically trained in that."

So here's a tip. Start cutting.

Self-made millionaires tend to make this list extremely short. They know that no one can focus on seven different talents. So leave out all but the three things you are best at. Choose those skills that you think you could convincingly

> *Write this down on a Post-it note and stick it here:*
>
> **My strengths are...**

explain to a total stranger, because that's what you'll need to do get rich: Sell other people on your value to them.

Next to each of these three top skills of yours, write down three clear statements that provide evidence that you do this well. "I do this faster and better than anyone I know." "I'm chosen to lead these kinds of projects at work." "I created a method at my company for this."

The more objective the evidence, like bonuses or tangible results you've reached, the better. Keep in mind that you may not realize what you're best at because whatever it is comes naturally to you.

#2. Catalog how each of these strengths commonly leads to wealth. Take this list of three things you do extremely well and write down the occupations that, to your knowledge, most often use those skills to make the most money.

Now ask yourself, *what kinds of people with those skills get rich?*

If you're a great cook, the richest cooks own restaurants, write cookbooks and have their own TV shows. If you're a great woodworker, the richest in your field run their own shops, do high-end custom work or leverage their skills to get into high-end real estate deals. And if you manage people well, the richest people in management always have a stake in the company they work for, no matter how big or small that business is.

These are the activities for which you are most likely to be well compensated, because the work you produce creates value for other people. The cookbook author helps the publisher make money. The woodworker on the real estate deal helps the developer sell the house for a premium price. The top manager helps grow the company's profits.

I've studied this with doctors, for instance. Of all the professions that require years of training, doctors on average are the highest paid. But the richest doctor is not the best doctor. The richest doctor is the one who first chose a specialty that pays very well and then took an ownership stake in a medical practice. The same goes for lawyers, engineers, and even academics and clergy. The richest are always the ones who are living their language in a way that creates the highest compensation.

And this is why. Many of you will feel a little sick when you go over your personal list of prospective business pursuits. Maybe you'll feel an ache in the pit of your stomach. Sure, you may love to cook, but the thought of running a restaurant makes you nauseous. You may love woodworking but hate the real estate game, and the people in it. And while managing people may be fun for you, the corporate ladder is a tough climb and running your own business seems like a big, fat headache.

Every self-made millionaire has faced challenges with that same ache in his or her stomach. The difference? Self-made millionaires take that ache as a signal that they need to go find some partners to take on these other tasks. For them, the ache in the pit of the stomach is a valuable source of information. It tells them that there's something they don't know how to do, that they're not good at. It's something that stands between them and their financial goals unless they can find someone else to help them. That's the point of the final part in Learning Your Language.

Write this down on a Post-it note and stick it here:

Which of my strengths lead to wealth?

#3. Make a long list of what you're not good at. Start by writing down the things that give you that ache when you consider what it might take to get rich at what you do best. You envision the headaches of running things. Write down how you're bad at managing people. You get hot flashes thinking of the paperwork. Write down that you're bad with numbers.

Remember how self-made millionaires tend to make a very short list of what they do best? Well, they're much more proficient at rattling off all the things they do badly.

A lot of people who wish they were rich are just too proud to admit they stink at some things. And not admitting what you stink at can really hold you back. There are only so many hours in a day. Waste your time with things you're bad at and you'll never get ahead.

Really great entrepreneurs are often very interesting people with a strong contradiction in their personalities. As a rule, they are very sure of themselves and may seem arrogant when they talk about what they know. But these same people will happily count off with no shame at all the many things they're terrible at.

"Entrepreneurs can seem very humble in some surprising ways," says Leann Mischel, a former corporate executive who now teaches entrepreneurship at Susquehanna University in Pennsylvania. "Over time, they get better at identifying what they don't do well, because they see positive results from handing those tasks over to true experts."

This list of what you do poorly is your list of what you must do less of, consciously, if you are ever going to meet your goals. These are the tasks and responsibilities you want to hand off to employees and partners. If you don't worry about them, you'll have more time to focus on what you do best. Eventually, you'll need to find the best people whose strengths complement your own. For now, just write down the list of all the things you do badly but that need to get done if you are going to succeed.

If the list has fewer than ten items, you need to try harder.

Write this down on a Post-it note and stick it here:

Which of my weaknesses prevent me from creating wealth?

If You Already Run Your Own Business...

Readers who are self-employed need to take a slightly different approach to Learning Your Language. In your case, you should start with #3. Make a long list of things related to your field that you know you don't do best. Then move on to #1 and #2. No matter what line of work you're in today, you still need to take that hard look at #2. That's what Learning Your Language is all about. You need to constantly question if what you're doing today and tomorrow is aligned with your long-term goal.

Every Field Has A Language

Some fields are more naturally inclined than others to offer lucrative business opportunities for people who've learned their language. But just about every profession offers opportunities for making millions, even those normally associated with academe and the nonprofit world. The profusion of charter schools in recent years, for instance, has made millionaires of many entrepreneurially minded teachers who likely took up the profession out of a love for teaching and the job security it offered.

Tom Schramski got a doctorate in psychology after growing up the son of a Minnesota gas station owner. He moved to Arizona and figured he'd set up a private practice. Then the state started contracting out the care of people with mental illnesses and disabilities. He and a partner started a company to compete for the contracts. Over 15 years, Community Psychology and Education Services grew to $5.5 million in revenues and Schramski ended up selling his company to his employees for $2.5 million.

You're Never Really Done Learning

As you make progress toward your goals and your vision, you should continue to reexamine which of your talents and skills are most likely to produce your next level of financial rewards. Learning Your Language is an ongoing task. Over time, Learning Your Language will become more and more about what you don't do than about what you do. Staying true to your language will help you peel away layer after layer of time-wasting activities and move your focus away from things that drain your time and energy. At its best, Learning Your Language will prompt you to delegate even some activities you are very good at, simply because you've found someone who does them even better.

From Our *Business Brilliant* Survey

"Setbacks and failures have taught me what I'm good at."

Self-made millionaires: 58 percent agree   Middle-class: 18 percent agree

---

More likely, though, Learning Your Language takes place when you evaluate what happened to a project that either went wrong or produced dismal results. Most self-made millionaires say that such disappointments help them determine which tasks they should keep within their direct control and which would be done better if handed off to others. This is what old-timers talk about when they say they attended the School of Hard Knocks.

To a large extent, Learning Your Language is an unavoidable process to rewire your brain for success. The discipline of evaluating your daily actions will almost certainly stir up a few unpleasant emotions. You might wonder why you engage in self-defeating behavior, why you keep wasting your time on one thing while avoiding the other thing most likely to put yourself in the line of money. You wonder why you just can't let go and admit that someone else is better suited for a given task.

Learning Your Language can also put you at risk of judging yourself too harshly and questioning whether you have what it takes to succeed. Try to remember that self-made millionaires confront those same issues and feel those same feelings. The difference is that they are more likely to put the self-judgment aside and use each negative feeling as a call to action.

For some, the process of Learning Your Language may even evoke a spiritual sense of fulfillment. If you want, you can consider finding your language as a way of more clearly defining your purpose on Earth. On the other hand, it can just as easily remind you that what you do best isn't necessarily what you enjoy doing the most. For these people, their language serves a different purpose. It can help them understand the degree of sacrifice that will be required in order to get rich. "It's not about doing what you love," says one entrepreneur. "It's doing what other people hate." He's right, of course. The fast food industry has spawned thousands upon thousands of self-made millionaire franchisees, not because the food is great, but because people hate to cook.

This is why learning your language works only after you've made that authentic decision to create wealth. It's a process that will show you where you need to compromise your sense of comfort and well-being in order to get what you want. If you've made the choice to get rich, you've already determined that the prospective rewards will be worth it.

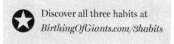
Step Three:
Create Your Exceptional Engine

You know how to make a living. Now you want to use your language to make a fortune.

So how do you get from the first place to the second?

With rare exceptions among born entrepreneurs, everyone starts out working for wages or a straight salary. Unless you went into sales right out of school, salaried labor is how most educated people begin their careers and learn the ropes. It's true of most self-made millionaires, too. Most used their years of salaried work to hone the skills and abilities that would later become the strengths that make up their language.

The difference is that at some point, all self-made millionaires made a critical leap. They transitioned from working for others by selling their time to working for themselves by selling results. Making this leap requires a set of four activities that spell out LEAP:

Learning. Earning. Assistance. Persistence.

LEAP is a framework that will be helpful to you at every stage of your development as a self-made millionaire. It can inform your business decisions. It can help shape a negotiating strategy. It can give focus to your networking plans. It can even help you prioritize your daily to-do list.

But at this initial stage of your journey—the one crucial to making your actual LEAP to profiting from your language—the tasks associated with LEAP should look something like this:

1. **Learn** more about the moneymaking opportunities nearest your language. Find a project that's on the more lucrative end of whatever you do best. Consider ways of investing your time in educating yourself about the

opportunities within your language. Make time during your lunch hour or even during your working day to learn more about where you want to go next.

2. **Earn** some cash using your language. Put your learning to use and get yourself in the line of money. Start exercising the part of your brain that attracts you to getting paid for results. At the start, you might make $500 but it takes you 50 hours to do it. Ending up with a minimum-wage result isn't so bad if you're refining your language. Earning—even if you're earning poorly—is part of the process when you're learning your language. Today, $500 is the best deal you can get for exercising your language. Try again and shoot for $5,000.

3. Get **Assistance** from people in your informal network. If you've developed any of the skills within your language, you already interact with a network of people who are more successful than you at what you do. Perhaps you've been too intimidated to approach them. If that's been your problem, now is the perfect time to get over it. Now you have vision and a goal. You have a purpose.

4. Exercise **Persistence** because once you're working within your language, nothing is more important than persistence. The people who succeed are usually the ones who make mistakes and learn from those experiences. That's why we've found that highly successful people fail about three times more often than do middle-class people with the same amount of education and experience. Try to remember that if this path were easy and risk-free, everyone would be doing it. All too often, middle-class people use one painful failure as an excuse for why they never tried to make their LEAP.

From Our *Business Brilliant* Survey

"I've typically given up and focused on other projects following a bad outcome."

Self-made millionaires: 2.3 percent   Middle-class: 54 percent

"I've typically tried again in the same field following a bad outcome."

Self-made millionaires: 77 percent   Middle-class: 13 percent

---

A special note on the "Assistance" part of LEAP. Many capable salaried workers have a particular problem with this one. They're embarrassed to impose on someone. They may feel foolish about trying to strike out on their own. Accessing assistance can be the crucial missing piece, because you can really knock yourself out trying to do something by yourself, telling yourself you're working within your language, when much of your time and effort are wasted doing things you're too embarrassed to ask for help with.

So here's the important point to remember. Seeking assistance is not the same as begging for help. You have to assume that the successful people in your field know all about LEAP, by whatever name they may call it. If they're successful, they're probably already living their language and they've figured out how to find good people to take up tasks outside of their language. This is how self-made millionaires think. When you ask them for advice and assistance, the gears in their heads will start turning—not about how they can help you, but how you might help yourself by helping them. They will likely ask how you might be able to help them with their goals—while starting out on your own.

Go back and read your Vision Post-it Promise and your Five-Year Goal Post-it Promise.

How am I going to do this?

You're going to make a transition plan to LEAP. You're going to use all four points of LEAP as a tool, to reach that first annual financial goal, that first ridgeline up the mountain of your vision. You can develop a plan to learn more, to try one new project, to seek out help and then to persist in the face of disappointment.

There are a thousand different ways to do this, depending on your skills and your area of expertise.

One good place to start? Your current employer.

The business world has never been as flexible as it is today. You may want to look at making that flexibility work for you. If, like so many Americans, you're worried that layoffs and cutbacks will soon give you a shove out the door, you might want to check and see if your current employer would prefer to pay you to do your job functions on a contract basis. Then you'll have your time outside the office to grow your client base.

Find out if your employer is willing to negotiate a deal that would cut costs at the company and give you your chance to LEAP.

Creep To Your LEAP

The more common way to LEAP is to start some moneymaking activity on the side. Most real estate professionals start out renting a few properties as a sideline. Real estate investing is a popular idea because it holds out the promise, embraced by the likes of 2millionblog.com in Step 2, that you can get rich and keep your day job. But if real estate wheeling and dealing isn't your language you may get yourself in trouble this way.

The tale of woe told by 2millionblog.com extends to his hapless management of his rental property. With more than $100,000 tied up in the property, his full year of rental income netted just $931 in 2008.

Why? Maintenance, property management fees and all the usual expenses. Then a burglar broke down the door to the rental house when no one was home. He had to hire a contractor to fix the door. The tenants complained they no longer felt safe in the house and wanted to move out. The young engineer/landlord was sympathetic. He let them out of the lease, only to learn the Raleigh property market had softened. He had to rent the property for $40 per month below what the previous tenants had paid.

There is a comment section to the blog, and here's what one seasoned Raleigh landlord wrote: "This 'robbery' story is a familiar one to me...I have had several staged 'robberies' over the years and it always coincides with a tenant's desire to move. I'm not saying your tenant was BS-ing you, but your story, on its face, seems odd."

It's pretty evident that "property management" is not this young engineer's language. He will never get rich in the real estate game by being such a soft touch. That's the problem with most get-rich schemes peddled to the American public. They pretend you can make lots of money by competing in fields—like stocks and real estate—against battle-hardened professionals.

For some people, though, I'm sure these get-rich programs work. Which people? Probably the people who, if they did the language-learning process, would find stock trading or real estate dealing among their special talents and abilities.

And plenty of self-made millionaires "creep to their LEAP" by working in their off hours, as Debra Lin did with Cookie Lee jewelry. The difference is that Lin never thought she'd get rich by continuing to sell jewelry on the side. She knew, even though it took years, that a LEAP was in her future.

Plenty of self-made millionaires have gotten there by biding their time before quitting their day jobs. Some incorporate their companies and hire full-time employees while they work full time elsewhere. For years, Mike Officer, the

CEO of Carlisle Wine Cellars in Northern California, has maintained a full-time job as a software programmer. Officer has a clear plan in mind—he wants to sell a share of the company to outside investors. Robert M. Parker, Jr., the dean of wine critics, has lauded Carlisle's Zinfandel as "magnificent," but the company still hasn't reached the scale and customer base to attract the big offer that Officer is looking for. So he remains at his programmer job until the time is right to LEAP.

LEAP, Or Get Pushed?

The second most common way to make the LEAP is to get pushed.

Thousands of management employees get laid off every year as a result of company mergers or retrenchments. A famous case of someone who was pushed into prosperity is Bernie Marcus, who was fired as a store manager at a small Southern California hardware chain. Marcus made up his mind to run his own store, and thanks in part to the expertise he'd developed from his previous employer, the store grew into what would become the nationwide The Home Depot chain.

Oftentimes, laid-off employees get a buyout or decide to cash out their 401(k)s, and then invest in a franchise operation. There are risks involved, like there are in any business venture, but the main risk I see commonly ignored is whether, after all those years in corporate employment, those people are really cut out for running that franchise.

In other words, if that new franchisee tried to find his or her language, would he or she come up with the same set of strengths necessary to run a successful Quiznos? Or a Jiffy Lube?

Sometimes, yes. Usually, no.

This is why I believe it's so important to start with your language. It's what you know. It's where your instincts are bound to work best. It's where you already have skills you can count on, expertise this is proven to be capable of making money.

Ohio's Dave Krueger was pushed to LEAP in a different way. His 13-year career in search-and-rescue work for the state was ended by a back injury. He used his knowledge of his field to start a company that sells survival kits for cars and boats. The product line for World Prep includes high-tech blankets made by NASA. After six years, gross sales at the company approached $2 million.

The expertise you develop on the job matters a lot in your ability to learn your language. Psychologists who study occupational performance have a rule of thumb that ten years of what they call "deliberate practice" will set you head and shoulders above most people in ability and expertise. This is why amateur part-time real estate investors and stock pickers fail so miserably. Their markets are very competitive. They will always lose out to the guy with ten or more years of deliberate practice and expertise.

But no matter what your proficiency in your language, you'll never reach your goal if you don't put yourself in the line of money. That's exactly what Colonel Sanders did when all he had left to his name was a recipe for southern fried chicken.

Discover all three habits at
BirthingOfGiants.com/3habits

Step Four:
Failure Makes Perfect

The success story of Colonel Sanders and his Kentucky Fried Chicken has been told many times, usually as a tale about the virtue of persistence. I'm repeating it here for a different reason. The way Colonel Sanders got rich illustrates what I think is a far more valuable point. Sanders always followed the money, or as I like to say, he kept himself "in the line of money" at all costs. Even when he was broke and living in his car, he never gave up the equity stake in his work. Persistence can claim credit for Colonel Sanders' success, but it was equity that made him a multi-millionaire.

Back in the early 1950s, Harland Sanders was a small-town Kentucky restaurateur with his own secret recipe for fried chicken. When a new interstate highway bypassed his restaurant, business dropped and Sanders was forced to auction off the property. Figuring he was too old to start over at a better location, Sanders became one of those people who learn their language only because they've been forced to. At age 65, he set out to sell his fried chicken recipe to other restaurateurs on the condition that he receive a percentage of the sales of chicken cooked with his recipe.

Through thick and thin, Sanders never abandoned this one stipulation, which would account for all the millions he would eventually make. That equity stake in his chicken recipe was a matter of principle for Sanders. If people were going to pay to eat his chicken, Sanders wanted his share of each sale. He was determined to follow the money on every drumstick and chicken breast cooked with his recipe.

The legend is that Sanders pitched his idea to more than 1,000 restaurants before he closed his first deal. No one will ever know the true number of his rejections, but no one disputes that Sanders started out in Kentucky and not one restaurateur took him up on his business proposition until he got to Utah two years later.

Sanders was convinced he had a multimillion-dollar recipe in his pocket, and he wouldn't part with it until its true value was realized. The recipe started earning him a fine livelihood once the Kentucky Fried Chicken franchise network took shape. But it took more than ten years before Sanders finally unlocked his recipe's full equity value with his sale of the company for $2 million.

This is why I recommend that whatever you do, and wherever you start out at, you need keep your eye on getting that equity stake when it comes to doing what you do best—using your language. Even if you are self-employed, you are unlikely to reach your ten-year goal unless you have an equity stake in your work that is potentially equal in value to that goal.

In other words, if your financial goal is to be worth $10 million, you need to be working on one or more projects in which your cumulative stakes potentially reach a value of $10 million or more. You're probably not there yet. You may not even be close. But before you start taking on projects and negotiating terms on those projects, you need to map out an income path that will take you to that point where the collective value of all your equity projects add up to your ten-year goal.

Colonel Sanders saw that income path for himself. He knew he needed a chain of restaurants serving his chicken before he could make a good living and be poised to have something worth selling. That's why from the start the Colonel held on to his equity stake in his chicken recipe as the non-negotiable linchpin to all his dealings. He always had a clear income path to his big payday.

Now, most of you reading this are not little old men living out of your cars with chicken recipes in your pockets. You've got lives and responsibilities to tend to. For most of you, your big equity play is still a figment of your imagination. Most of you reading this will not be working tomorrow on the thing that will make you rich ten years from now.

It's important, though, that you work toward that end today. It's just as important that you avoid chasing schemes today that will only lead you away from it. So before you even try to determine what kind of projects you want to take on, you need to map out the general income path you want to take to equity and your ten-year goal. You won't be ready to start picking projects and negotiating terms until you've set your own ideal path for following the money.

1. Get Paid For Results

Now that we've dealt with the tremendous importance of equity, let's put it aside for a moment. Let's focus instead on how to make a living in a way that takes you toward equity and will eventually make you rich.

You've identified your vision, your goals and your language. Now you need to find ways to put them all to work for you in the line of money.

Wherever value gets created in the business activities that come as a result of you living your language, that's the line of money. Wherever and whenever the money moves, that's where you want to be.

A restaurant owner sells a $25 plate of pasta that costs $4 to make. Whatever is left of that $21, after all the bills are paid, belongs to the restaurant owner. A retailer sells a shirt for $40 that cost $12 wholesale. The $28 difference belongs to the retailer. A landlord rents an apartment for $2,100 a month, but the mortgage on the unit is only $1,000 a month. It's up to the landlord to figure out how much of the $1,100 difference he can keep for himself.

The restaurateur, the retailer and the landlord weren't paid for their work. They were rewarded for their results. That's what I call being in the line of money.

If you want to be rich, you need to be part of any team that claims the reward when your prices stay high and your costs run low. When money changes hands, when someone is happy to pay $10,000 for a thing that cost only $5,000 to produce, you want to be the producer.

Who is outside the line of money? Millions of wage workers and salaried employees. Generally speaking, employees opt out of the line of money because there's always the risk of losing money in the line of money. Instead, workers trade away that risk. They agree to become just a fixed cost in someone else's line-of-money equation.

You don't need to operate a physical asset like a store or a restaurant to be in the line of money. Those are just the kinds of operations where the line of money is easiest to illustrate.

The line of money exists wherever goods and services are exchanged. Every time a financial transaction takes place, someone is in the line of money, positioned to come out on top in the exchange. You want to take a look at your language now and consider what you can do in order to be that person.

2. Climb the Line-of-Money Ladder

Let's break things down a little. There are a handful of different ways to be in the line of money, and some are more lucrative than others. Once you have an idea of the kind of work you're best suited for, then you're ready to look at the line of money as it runs upward toward equity, like a ladder with four rungs.

Each rung on the Line-of-Money Ladder is defined by your mode of compensation, and each rung demands higher risks and yields higher rewards than the rung below it.

Whichever rung you think you belong on, it's important to be mindful about the one you want to reach for next. It's also helpful to look at the rung you want to move up from. You'll see that even at the bottom rung, merely being in the line of money gives you many more opportunities to climb the ladder than you will ever have while working for a salary.

The Line-of-Money Ladder

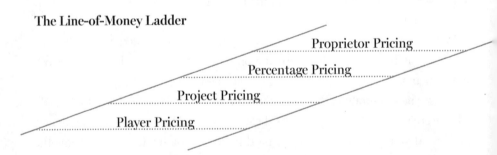

Proprietor Pricing

Percentage Pricing

Project Pricing

Player Pricing

The Lowest Rung: Player Pricing

The bottom rung on the Line-of-Money Ladder is occupied by self-employed consultants and other independent contractors who sell their time at an hourly rate. Hourly consultants don't really stand to reap rewards when money changes hands. They don't get paid for results like the landlord or the restaurateur. For that reason, these people are only nominally in the line of money. It's difficult, if not impossible, to get rich if you're compensated only in this way. Your time, after all, is finite. There is a limit to how much revenue you can make on your own.

On the other hand, if you can manage to subcontract some of your workload, you can start making money beyond the boundaries of your own time. And if you do well enough that demand for your services exceeds your supply of hours, you can bid up your prices. Think of the most highly paid trainers, psychoanalysts or other personal service professionals with elite clients.

Best of all, if you find yourself in that kind of seller's market for your services, you have room to negotiate better terms. You can ask for other forms of compensation that put you on a higher rung of the Line-of-Money Ladder. If you have a skill that's in demand and you know where you want to go with it, Player Pricing is not a bad place to start.

The Middle Rungs:

Project Pricing

When you accept pay by the project, you enjoy the advantage of being paid for a result, regardless of your time commitment. You always run the risk that a project will take longer than you thought, but you've also got a powerful incentive to finish the job quickly.

Project Pricing shares the same downside as Player Pricing, however, in that you don't get a share of any of the profits you may help create. For that reason alone, this rung of the ladder is still unlikely to yield the long-term financial success you want.

Percentage Pricing

When you work for a percentage of profits on a project, you're finally positioned in the line of money to enjoy a share of the rewards of success. There's no guarantee you'll make more money this way, but you can approach new projects of this kind on the basis of potential earnings, instead of the cash flow that Project Pricing and Player Pricing provide.

Many Project Pricing deals have a Percentage Pricing component worked in, almost like a bonus for helping a winning effort. When we get to negotiating later in the book, you'll see how you can trade off a little money up front in order to get a bigger piece of the back end—a cut of the proceeds once the project succeeds.

The Top Rung: Proprietor Pricing

Equity ownership is the top rung of the Line-of-Money Ladder. It is the highest achievement in the world of wealth and it should be the ultimate goal of everyone who wants to get rich. You want an ownership stake—either as a sole proprietor or in a partnership—of something that you can build and sell at many times its rate of annual earnings.

As I pointed out before, nearly all the self-made millionaires in our survey believe equity is essential to getting rich. Our survey also found that about 85 percent of the self-made millionaires either have or had a substantial equity stake in a business venture. And about half of the remaining group, the ones without equity today, say they're seeking it.

You have to remember, though, that ownership and equity are not identical. Plenty of businesses are successful on a cash-flow basis—they make money—but they build little or no equity for their owners. Restaurants, for instance, rarely build equity beyond the value of the real estate they occupy. That's because it's too easy for someone to duplicate the success of your restaurant without paying you anything. All your landlord needs to do is wait until your lease is up and then continue your business without you.

So as you begin to develop your income path to your goal, you need to consider this potential pitfall. Equity holds great potential value when it represents an accomplishment that is not easily duplicated. Those restaurants, for example, may be poor equity plays, but any restaurateur can reverse that by owning the real estate the restaurant is housed in or developing a food preparation process that's hard to duplicate. In these cases, purchasing the business may be more attractive than trying to duplicate its success.

A survey of small-business owners by *Inc.* magazine once showed that 41 percent started their businesses with a clear idea of an exit strategy. These smart businesspeople started out from day one looking to create a business that would be worth selling someday.

That's the smart way to do it. As you figure out the kind of equity play or plays you want to pursue in working toward your ten-year-goal, the nuanced

---

From Our *Business Brilliant* Survey

"I have (or have had) a substantial equity position in a business venture."

99 percent of self-made multimillionaires

85 percent of self-made millionaires

10 percent of middle-class survey respondents

---

quality of equity will become clearer to you.

You want to build something that possesses a financial life of its own. That's what gives your equity value. It can go on without you. It can produce income for the next owner far into the future. Is it any wonder so many small-business owners call their businesses their "babies"?

Climbing the Line-of-Money Ladder is not a linear process. It's very common for self-made millionaires to be involved in a broad mix of projects. Some are player-priced or project-priced for their cash-generating qualities. Others, with higher risks or longer-term payoffs, are priced on a percentage or equity basis. Keeping a healthy mix of projects on the various rungs of the ladder is a smart way to hedge your bets against financial disaster should one of the riskier projects fail.

A good way to look at the Line-of-Money Ladder is this: When you're starting out, Player Pricing and Project Pricing are the surest way to maintain your current income. It's how you stay in the game, and perhaps move incrementally toward your goals. Percentage Pricing is how you enhance your wealth and start meeting your short-term financial goals. Proprietor Pricing—equity participation— is how you create new wealth. That's how you will ultimately reach your long-term vision of wealth.

3. Set Out Your Income Path

So how do you put the Line-of-Money Ladder to work for you? It's time to make a map of your future income path.

In the chart that follows, name three activities that revolve around your language that you might want to pursue on each rung of the Line-of-Money Ladder.

Start out with Player Pricing. Name three types of jobs that require the skills and talents within your language for which you can hire yourself out on a hourly basis. If you've got computer skills, it might be a variety of jobs related to setting up networks or custom programming. I know people who get paid to load CDs onto iPods. Whatever these jobs are, they're your language. Write them down.

Now, consider the inherent limitations in that list. How much can you really charge per hour for these tasks? If you don't know, look around. The whole point of this exercise is to focus your thinking and educate yourself so you'll be ready for the next step toward creating wealth.

Once you've grasped the earning potential of working by the hour, you're ready to consider Project Pricing. What kinds of jobs would require you to step up and propose a project for a flat-rate fee? If it's something you can't do alone, educate yourself about what it costs to hire someone on an hourly basis in your field. Now write down your three possible project types.

Now it's time to consider Percentage Pricing—the icing on the cake of Project Pricing. What kind of project do you think would create so much value for a client that he or she would be willing to pay you a percentage of the proceeds? Think in terms of helping build something that's going to sell. It's not easy, but use your imagination. Who in your field is making money this way? Look it up. Ask around. You may be surprised by what you find, which, again, is the whole point of the exercise.

Finally, write down your three most likely equity plays, from where you stand now. Some of you are already there. You've got an equity stake in something already. For you, it's time to list the three equity plays that put you clearly within striking distance of your five-year goal or your ten-year vision. You want to make $5 million selling this business, $2 million selling that property and $3 million selling some other thing—all of which adds up to your $10 million goal.

For everyone else, for whom equity is still several steps away, try to study the nine projects you've already listed on the lower rungs of the Line-of-Money Ladder. Try to imagine how you can build on these successes, go into partnerships with the people you've worked with. The entire LEAP program is designed around building a network of people who know and like your work, so you've got ready partners to go with to the next level. So write down the three types of equity plays you can realistically envision for yourself, based on the work you're most likely to do further up the ladder.

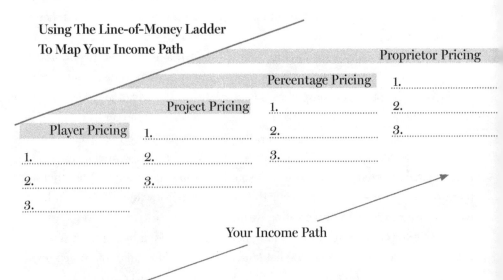

Using The Line-of-Money Ladder To Map Your Income Path

Proprietor Pricing
1. ....
2. ....
3. ....

Percentage Pricing
1. ....
2. ....
3. ....

Project Pricing
1. ....
2. ....
3. ....

Player Pricing
1. ....
2. ....
3. ....

Your Income Path

When you're done, you'll have ideas for 12 projects, arrayed from lowest value to highest value, each building on those that come before it. You've mapped your future income path.

Climbing the Line-of-Money Ladder from Player Pricing to an equity sale is a proven way to wealth. In one of my previous books, I told the story of a San Antonio-based financial advisor who, like a lot of financial advisors, was making a fine living. He was working way too hard at it, though, and the future promised only more of the same.

Like most financial advisors, he was paid a commission on whatever financial products he was able to sell to his clients. To maintain his relationship with those clients, he provided them with a lot of financial services at no charge. He had to keep 1,200 accounts just to maintain his income. Since financial advising is a relatively easy field to enter, his practice held no equity value at all.

So he decided to take all the skills and expertise he'd developed to a new level. He changed his firm to a "wealth management" practice and moved up the ladder to Percentage Pricing. Wealth managers work for a flat percentage of assets under management. If a client's net worth climbs in a given year, the wealth manager shares in that growth.

Becoming a wealth manager, however, involved taking a big risk. Almost none of his 1,200 clients had enough money to be worthy of managing on a percentage basis. He had to let go of all but 17 of them. Those were his richest clients, and then he had to set about finding dozens of other clients with similar levels of wealth.

It was difficult work with no assurance of success, and he used every point of LEAP to achieve it. But in less than two years he was making three times as much money and had cut his work hours in half.

That wasn't the end of the story. His new wealth management practice was a true accomplishment. With 80 wealthy clients and an annual cash flow of about $800,000, it had equity value. This practice was not something easily duplicated. Unlike his financial advising firm, this wealth management practice could sell for many times its annual earnings. And when he decided to sell it, he made millions.

Does this seem daunting? Consider the fact that in every field where money changes hands—even in the so-called nonprofit sector—there are people in the line of money getting rich.

In every field, there are similar ways to climb the ladder from Player Pricing to profit participation to equity.

Many self-made millionaires have started out as player-priced professionals in law, accounting and other skilled occupations. They got tired of getting paid high hourly wages to make other people rich. Instead, they started trading their professional capabilities for equity in the deals.

This same dynamic happens in a lot of fields—most fields, really. Smart college professors in business and the sciences are often involved in similar equity plays in which their expertise makes them a key player on the team. Even in the public service sector—among public safety and schoolteachers—you will find some that have taken their years of training (at public expense) and turned that experience into valuable equity deals.

In all these public-sector fields, the for-profit sale of equipment and educational materials are a multibillion-dollar industries. The Line-of-Money Ladder in these areas is enormous, and there are former civil servants with equity stakes in all those businesses.

Working within your language and earning money by doing that is a habit shared by every successful person I've ever met. Your current career path is no obstacle to success. It's merely the starting point on your Ladder and your income path.

Now you have your roadmap for learning your language, and with that, you possess the same knowledge that the most successful people in the world have. All that remains is for you to put your language into action. In *Step One: You Need a Plan*, I wrote that the basic simplicity of this process would stop most people from putting these ideas into action for themselves. Learning your language isn't a stock tip. It's not even a secret. It's information that's plainly available for you to access, apply and refine. The choice is all yours.

But wait, there's more!

Like the old hucksters of infomercial TV, there's always more. In this case, I've shared with you the first habit. There are two other essential habits that will assist you in achieving your goals. Again, no reason to keep secrets here. In fact, not only are the other two not secrets (I've already mentioned them in this book several times), they're freely available to anyone who chooses to access them.

To learn all three habits and how they create a synergistic system that can change the path of your life, go to poweredbyben.com/3habits. From there, I'll tell you everything I've learned after a lifetime of interviewing the most successful people on Earth.

poweredbyben.com/3habits

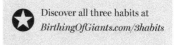
Your Post-it Roadmap

Learn Your Language

Your LEAP This Week

Learning: What new information do you need to find out this week about your language?

Earning: What crucial action are you going to take this week speaking from your center?

Assistance: What kind of help (outside of your own language) are you going to seek out or leverage this week?

Persistence: What are you going to try to do this week that has failed for you in the past?

Your LEAP This Month

Name three measurable results you're going to achieve this month for each LEAP activity.

Learning:

Earning:

Assistance:

Persistence:

Your LEAP This Year:

Name three measurable results you're going to achieve in the next 12 months for each LEAP activity.

Learning:

Earning:

Assistance:

Persistence:

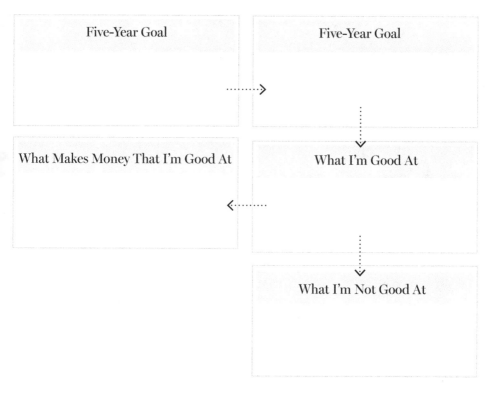

Five-Year Goal	Five-Year Goal
What Makes Money That I'm Good At	What I'm Good At
	What I'm Not Good At

What Comes Next:
A Decision That Could Change Your Life

Something happens when you finally discover your language. You want to talk about it, explore it, share it. I've built my business around my language, and I'm also passionate about helping others do the same. So here's what could come next for you:

Over 20 years, I've worked with every kind of business owner and every type of business model you can think of: business-to-business, business-to-consumer, B2B2C, B2G, you name it, I've coached it through our **Birthing of Giants Fellowship Program**. After doing it for so long, I made a discovery: there is such a thing as a "perfect business." In fact, one day, an entrepreneur presented this perfect business model at our Fellowship Program at Massachusetts Institute of Technology (MIT). It was on the fifth day of our 5-day program and I'll never forget it. Myself and all of the Board of Experts of Birthing of Giants were speechless. We had nothing to add. It was...perfect. And now it's well on the way to becoming a nine-figure business (that's more than $100 million, FYI).

Now that you know more about your language, it's time to pair that with a great business model. More than anything, these two elements (your language and a great business model) create entrepreneurial success.

Head over to our online video training for "The Perfect Business Model" and take the LEAP! I'll see you there...**birthingofgiants.com/pbm**

With gratitude,

Lewis Schiff

About Lewis Schiff

Lewis Schiff is the chairman of the Birthing Of Giants Fellowship Program, an entrepreneur's education program for owners of fast-growing companies. Apply to be a Birthing of Giants Fellow at *BirthingOfGiants.com*.

Schiff is also the author of the best-selling book *Business Brilliant: Surprising Lessons from the Greatest Self-Made Business Icons*, which focuses on the wealth-creating behaviors and attitudes that work best in the new economy (Harper Collins 2013) and features in-depth profiles of the success philosophies of entrepreneurial greats such as Richard Branson and Steve Jobs.

In 2010, Schiff founded **Inc. Magazine's Business Owners Council**, a membership organization for top entrepreneurs and owners of closely held family businesses. Speakers to The Council membership include former U.S. Treasury Secretary Hank Paulson, Howard Schultz of Starbucks, Deepak Chopra, and Jim McCann, founder of 1-800-Flowers.

Schiff has co-authored two books: *The Influence of Affluence: How the Rich Are Changing America* (2006) charts the rise of America's growing affluent middle class through original research and analysis, and *The Armchair Millionaire* (2000) describes a wealth-creation system that leverages Nobel Prize-winning methodologies.

Schiff has sold two media businesses to publicly-traded companies.

CPSIA information can be obtained
at www.ICGtesting.com
Printed in the USA
LVHW031115060422
715474LV00002B/215

9 781312 608672